AND SARAH LAUGHED

AND SARAH LAUGHED

BETTER NOT BITTER

BY

JANNIE WEST-MAYS

XULON PRESS

Xulon Press
2301 Lucien Way #415
Maitland, FL 32751
407.339.4217
www.xulonpress.com

Unless otherwise indicated, Scripture quotations taken from the King James Version (KJV)–*public domain.*

Printed in the United States of America.

ISBN-13: 978-1-5456-7353-9

CREDITS

In loving memory of:
Deacon William A. Watson, Sr.
Mother Cornelia H. Watson
Reverend Dr. James Hallman
Mother Lois Hallman
Special thanks to
My colleagues:
Dr. Ira Gerald
Deaconess Marion Fleming
Ms. Sandra Hassan
My children
Eartley L. West, Jr.
Wayne A. West
Harold C. West, Sr.
Allen L. West
Durwood Cox, Jr.
Lasetta Simeona
Erik Townsend
Loretta T. Wilson
Meilee Bartley

TABLE OF CONTENTS

FOREWORD

Dr. Ira Gerald

I remember meeting Jannie Mays, some twenty years ago. At that time, she was known as Miss West. She was working as a social studies teacher in the Roosevelt Jr.- Sr. High School and administrator for the adult education program where she was famous for being a strict teacher and a disciplinarian. She had a presence. I was recommended to her by the superintendent of schools to interview for a teaching position to work under her supervision in the night school for adults who were preparing for their GED exams. Upon meeting her for the first time, I was a little nervous. She was clearly confident and serious about education. Her appearance was one of a traditional church lady, sort of like a grandmother type of figure. One would know immediately that she demanded respect, and after getting to know her, we would realize that she had earned it. Little did I know at the time that although her appearance and style of dress was accurate in its depiction of a church lady and a mother figure, which she was both, she would be so very approachable and wise in her counsel.

Soon after our initial meeting, we became the best of friends. I have had countless dinners at her house. We have worshipped together, performed community service together, and travelled the country to one church venue or another, enjoying many, many, occasions in what she and I have come to call "The Black Religious Experience." As the years progressed since our first conversation, I have found her to be a well of wisdom and a friend indeed. I had no idea Jannie would end up fulfilling so many roles in my life, a mother figure, role model, best friend, and my chit-chat buddy. During our many countless conversations, she would tell me stories about her life that I found fascinating. She told me that she wanted to write a book about her life and how blessed she has been down through the years.

Finally, the book that I have been hearing about for over five years is now available for all of us to read, enjoy, and benefit from. This book is written by my dear friend, Jannie Mays. Some may know her as a minister of the Christian Gospel or a teacher par excellence, administrator, mother or auntie, I just call her blessed. I am sure that in reading this book, your life will be enriched, and you will leave each chapter smiling and finding emotional bridges as we reflect on our lives' journeys. I am excited to read each word of encouragement through her experiences that she shares so generously through these pages. I know that this book will be a blessing to each and every reader and leave us longing for more of these pearls of wisdom. I am eternally grateful to have her as a friend, and I join you with excitement as we turn the pages slowly and ponder how good God has been to each of us. Each page is filled with words that bring hope, truth, and enlightenment that can only come by years of experience and grace. Thank you, Mother, for sharing your story with the world. Truly the world is a better place because of your life and your sharing.

INTRODUCTION

In January 1970, my life took what I now consider a nose-dive. I was the young mother of two boys, Eartley Levi West, Jr., and Wayne Albert West, ages four and five. I soon discovered that number three, Harold Cornelius West, was on his way. My situation could not have been any worse, or at least that was the way it looked at that time. I was married in 1965, and in 1970 I was among the ranks of the single parents, pregnant, unskilled, and working as a domestic. However, I do not recall being uneasy, frightened, or afraid of the future.

This was what I did know: I was directly responsible for two other human beings, and in a few months, it would be three others and me. I also know that it was the faith that my parents had taught me by the example of their lives. Christian families raised their children according to Bible scriptures such as in the Book of Esther when the enemy proposed the extermination of the Jewish nation. Esther followed the instructions of Mordecai and she and her maidens fasted and prayed, and God spared the Jewish people.

That was over forty-eight years ago, and the story has a very interesting and a happy ending.

As life unfolded for me, I began to experience uncommon favor in all areas of my life. I mentioned being a domestic worker. I also provided childcare services as well as serving private dinner parties. I gained a stellar reputation in all areas, I was sought after, and I was always busy. I was able to attend college thru a fully funded program and was also given childcare.

Despite all the problems that I faced over the years, I remained active in my spiritual life. Ministry is and always has been the center of my life. I attended worship services, Sunday school and Bible study on a weekly basis. It is my hope that as you read my story you will see that the hand of God was on my life. If you have lost hope, it is my prayer that my story will inspire you and that you will find new strength to follow and chase your dreams. If you are like me, now living my dream life, I encourage you to inspire others and let success become contagious.

I use the phrase "I am excited," because daily I am literally blown away as the blessings of God overtake my family. For instance, in August 2018, my brother, who is also my pastor, was consecrated a Bishop in the Apostolic Faith Church of God Live On, which is the movement that we grew up in. Our parents were among the founding members of the movement.

When my # 3, son, Harold West Sr., who is now forty-eight years old, informed me that his mother-in-law, Reverend Regina Johnson was opening the Hi Hello Childcare center, and I was summoned to become the director, I am not sure how I reacted. Look at me, seventy-four years old, retired for five years. I did not know what was going on. For the first time,

I was scared and I was not sure if I had the stamina to undertake such an important project. However, I quickly adjusted, and I loved to work with the young people.

As you will see as you read on, there were always people in my life who were there to assist me, no matter what the task consisted of.

I am a product of very humble beginnings. I grew up in Virginia with my parents and six brothers and sisters. Meager is the way I would describe my lifestyle. We always had enough housing, food, and clothing; however, we did not know that we were really poor.

My major break came in 1974, when I heard the term "free college." That was enough to get me stirred up. New York had the Higher Education Opportunity Program, HEOP, for disadvantaged students. I was happy when I was recruited by Molloy College to enter the program as a student. It was a great experience; it was secular education and cultural awareness. Having been raised in the segregated south, my interaction with other races had been limited. Also, the Pentecostal faith was very strict; my exposure to life as I know it today was nonexistent. The HEOP program provided me more than an education. It was a total transformation and I am so grateful for the experience and the doors that were opened for me because I have a college degree.

I began my journey in the field of education as a substitute teacher and continued as a social studies teacher, adult education, teacher/director, assistant principal, and pre-kindergarten director. After five years in pre-K, I finished my career as assistant principal in the Roosevelt Middle School on June

30, 2011. I encountered some problems along the way, but you will see that I won the battle.

The Head Start Program was the second part of a twofold blessing for me. It was now 1974, and my child born in 1970 was now four years old and I consider to this day that he was and is a blessing to me. Childcare was expensive and was not provided by social services if you were in a four-year college program. With Harold's birth came a floodgate of blessings. Remember the nosedive that I mentioned? Well, my life took a strange turn. Not only was I able to complete my education, I also became involved in The Community Action Program and also the Day Care Council. These two venues allowed me to attend workshops and learn about policy making as it related to providing services to public. I have been able to assist others over the years with my experiences as a member of certain committees.

Overall, I have been blessed with good health. In my early years, I had very few health problems. At this present time, I take several medications, but I am considered in good health for my age.

Finally, it is my hope that if you are about to give up hope and throw in the towel because of life's unfortunate circumstances, as you read this account of my life, just know that God has not forgotten you. When Sarah thought that being a mother was impossible, God blessed her in her old age.

Chapter 1

HI HELLO: HOW DID I GET HERE?

So Sarah laughed to herself as she thought,
"After I am worn out and my lord is old, will I now
have this pleasure?"
–Genesis 18:12, NIV[1]

When you look at the life of Sarah, you might wonder why she was not content with her life, and then you remember that this is the twenty-first century. In Sarah's days, a woman's worth was tied to her ability to have a male child. Barrenness was a curse. Sarah had a life of great material wealth as the wife of Abraham, but after a substantial time, she had not given him a son, and she was grieved because of this.

She took matters into her own hands and gave Hagar, her servant, to Abraham to bear a son. There was just one problem: Ishmael. The son of Hagar and Abraham was not the son of the promise. As life unfolded, Sarah was loved by her husband and worshiped with him as he moved from place to place. One day, when they were both old, past childbearing age, Abraham had some visitors who appeared to be ordinary men. However, they were divine messengers. Abraham asked Sarah to fix them something to eat. Sarah complied, but she was also a typical woman. She was listening to their conversation, and when one of them told Abraham that they were going to become parents, she laughed. I believe that Sarah's response was normal, and I would have reacted in the same manner.

It is traditional that a seventeen or eighteen-year-old high school graduate fills out several college applications and waits for responses. One makes a choice and usually spends the next four years in undergraduate studies, until around twenty or twenty-one years of age. That was not the scenario for me. In 1960, I could not even imagine that college was in my future because of my economic status. Life was never stagnant for me. I never had pity parties and I made the best of any situation that I found myself in. Sarah followed all the rules and mandates of her day; mainly she was strong in her faith in Almighty God. Like Sarah, my faith in God remained strong even when I did not see a bright future. I never lost hope and now I realize that my dream was delayed but not denied.

Fourteen years after high school, I went to college to become an elementary school teacher. After college, my career took a turn in a completely opposite direction, and I ended up as a social studies teacher at Roosevelt Jr.-Sr. High School. I enjoyed every minute in the classroom. Being a very strong disciplinarian helped me create a positive learning environment.

Throughout my own life (I am in my seventies at the time of this writing), often my professional life was going well, but most of the time my personal life was in shambles. I was able to overcome, however, because I wrapped myself up in my work and the care of my children. My children gave me purpose and kept me focused. Life was a struggle, and I knew only the strong would survive. So, after a successful career, I retired and sat daily with other retired seniors, and we proved that where there is life, there is hope. God can revive, rejuvenate, and give life—even when it looks hopeless...and Sarah laughed.

In September 2016, I came out of retirement to assist a family member who was establishing a daycare center: the Hi Hello Center at 212 S. Ocean Avenue, Freeport, New York. I had turned seventy-four in August and had been happily retired from being a public-school administrator for five years. My only work since then had been as a substitute teacher, and that was for only a few days once in a while during the school year. The idea of me holding a full-time job again was unreal. However, for the next nine months, I reported to my assignment as director of the daycare and was shocked that I really enjoyed it. The other ladies who worked there were sixty-four-year-old Graciela Elizabeth Alford, office manager; seventy-four-year-old Elnora Martin, office assistant; and sixty-nine-year-old Rev. Regina Johnson, owner of the center. Rev. Johnson and Elizabeth Alford arrived first, to receive the children, ranging in age from six weeks to five years old, who were being dropped off by their parents. Although there were times when some children experienced separation anxiety, we always greeted them with smiles and welcoming arms.

The interesting part, however, was that I began to ask myself some questions: How did I get here? Why am I here? The answers to these questions are very complex.

Hi Hello, was acquired by the Deeper Life Fellowship and Deliverance Center in November of 2015. There was much joy and excitement surrounding the acquisition. The strong leader, Rev. Johnson, and members of the congregation rallied together and raised the capital for this project. Why was I chosen? There are two reasons: (1) Over twenty-five years ago, Pastor Regina and I sat together and shared our vision of providing an education for children of all ages; (2) Now, as grandmothers with three adult children, we knew we must follow the family tradition and work together to make our dream come true.

I quickly adjusted to my new job, although at first I was not sure I had the stamina to handle the daily routine. However, I began to enjoy the fast pace of each day and soon felt as if I had never left my previous position. Daily activities were stimulating. My own excitement surprised me, but then I remembered the years I was a childcare provider for private families, and later director of a public school pre-kindergarten center.

I arrived at Hi Hello with a wealth of information and experience. For example, my experience had taught me that there is power in music. One of my first actions was to program my computer for children's songs. When their behavior was bad or they experienced discomfort, I would play music. Soon, all would become calm.

Our year began with a very successful ribbon cutting ceremony. The staff and parents were great. Our days were filled with so many activities. We went on field trips to the theater and Hicks Nursery and always participated in fundraising activities. The highlights of that first year were an awards banquet and the first graduation ceremony. After a really nice graduation ceremony at the Free Will Baptist Church in Freeport, New York, I resigned from my position as director on June 16, 2017. What a wonderful end to an exciting year. Life comes in cycles and God knows what we need and when we need it.

There is no good thing that He will withhold from us. My favorite scripture is Psalm 92:12-14. It tells us this:

*The righteous flourish like the palm tree,
and grow like a cedar in Lebanon. They
are planted in the house of the Lord, they
flourish in the courts of our God.
They will bring forth fruit in old age, they
shall be filled with vitality and foliage.* [2]
*Then Isaac sowed in that land, and received
in the same year an hundred times: and the
LORD blessed him.* Genesis 26:12[3]

Early Life in Virginia

I was born the third child of Deacon Albert Watson and Mother Cornelia Hansley Watson on August 16, 1942, in Portsmouth, Virginia, during World War II. We were a traditional family, and my parents worked hard to support us and keep the family together. During this period, when food was rationed, my mother did not always have enough stamps to purchase food, but she said, "I have the baby."

Food Rationing in Wartime America–HISTORY ***
www.history.com/news/food-rationing-in-wartime-america
Food Rationing in Wartime America. On January 30, 1942, the Emergency Price Control Act granted the Office of Price Administration (OPA) the authority to set price limits and ration food and other commodities in order to discourage hoarding and ensure the equitable distribution of scarce resources. [4]

I was educated in the Portsmouth Public School System, but I do not have a lot of distinct memories of my elementary years. The first school I attended was Mount Hermon Elementary School, which was in the neighborhood. I do, however, remember that my first-grade teacher was Mrs. Bessie Smith and my second grade teacher was Mrs. Williams. Two others were Mrs. Brown and Mrs. Lindsey. I do remember my mother being a very supportive parent. She took an active parental role, in that I could volunteer her when my teacher would ask for room mothers. Today, I think that we might refer to them as community liaisons. We always had limited resources, but mother would always find a way to provide for us to participate in school activities such as May Day and other parent-teacher activities. My mother was a true role model and she set the standards very high for her girls and others to follow. My mother had great wisdom and she never let her economic circumstances determine her lifestyle. She was extremely creative and she sought to raise her children to first love God and to encourage them to aim for the sky.

In grades seven and eight, I attended Riddick Weaver Junior High School in downtown Portsmouth, Virginia. I felt that the teacher did not like me, but I loved school and tried to be a good student. As a ninth grader, I enrolled in I.C. Norcom High School in Portsmouth and remained there until the second semester of the tenth grade.

Home ownership had always been a priority for my family. Due to the efforts of Bishop Jesse Handshaw, a self-made contractor, who arranged for the financing, my family was able to move from the Jeffrey Wilson Projects to our own home on the outskirts of Portsmouth. At that time, I entered Crestwood High School. Although the school was great, there were some bumps and few opportunities for black students, but there were more successes than issues. I participated in extra-curricular activities, including the Journalism Club. When I graduated in 1960, my thoughts were about the future. Fortunately, my break in education did come fourteen years later in New York.

Church was the center of our lives. During those days, when you followed the Pentecostal tradition, almost all activities, including sports, were prohibited, unlike the liberality of today. I do not recall having a school social life, but I do not recall being bored. I guess I had too many siblings. One of the highlights of our lives was the Fifth Sunday Union. Our family was very visible. Our parents were founding members of the Apostolic Faith Live in 1952.

Some members of our family had musical talent; others had oratorical ability. My mother encouraged us to participate on programs when called upon. I taught my five-year-old sister, Annie, to recite the sixty-six books of the Bible. She became the highlight of any program going forward.

The Sunday School Union consisted of several churches of our denomination. We enjoyed the fellowship because of the opportunity to make friends with other young people. Convocations and conventions were also a part of our social and spiritual growth. Our mother taught us to love and to study the Word of God. She showed us by example how to be visible. Mother was a great Bible scholar and a wonderful teacher who was creative and innovative. She developed a program for children attending the convention and other large gatherings because she believed that children should not be left alone unsupervised. Her efforts are kindly remembered today by some of the young people with whom she worked. During my mother's funeral in 2004, people made remarks in the service regarding Mother's diligence and love of teaching, and also that she carried candy and other goodies.

We enjoyed school vacations. During the summer, Mother would sign us up for the local Vacation Bible Schools. We attended at least two or three every summer. She also signed us up for activities in the local parks, where I remember learning arts and crafts. Also, at some time during the summer, we would visit our relatives in Wilmington, North Carolina. Remember, our lives in Virginia were primarily church-centered. We loved our North Carolina trips because they included trips the beach and other fun activities rather than church.

Although our home was always lacking in style and flair, we always had a roof over our heads and food to eat. We never realized that we were poor. Our home was always a haven for others. We always had visitors. Our parents were so compassionate. Mother was quiet, but serious. She was in charge of the family. Daddy never made a decision. He would answer our requests by saying, "Ask your mother."

Daddy was a great entertainer, he could remember stories about almost any subject, and he would talk for hours. We did not have a television or a radio when we were growing up. We had no phone until later years. Sometime, probably years later, a neighbor would have a telephone and everyone in the neighborhood would use their telephone. Daddy was a great provider, because his own father left a lot to be desired. He loved and supported his children. He was a very generous man and he taught us that a life of service to mankind is a blessed life.

Our active and visible church lives required an adequate wardrobe for local services and the annual general assembly, known as the Convention. We learned to stretch our already limited funds. As time passed, we became very good at making our own clothes. Marion was the best seamstress. I came in second. We would start weeks ahead of the convention working on our wardrobes. We were known for fashion. At one gathering, someone said, "I wonder what the Watson Sisters will be wearing today." Mother often dressed us alike as children. We continue to do the same thing today.

My sixth-grade teacher, Mr. Goodrich, wanted to follow me home because of my misbehavior in school. I misled him or ducked, probably ran ahead of him. He was able to contact my parents anyway. That was the only time in my life that I remember my father disciplining me with physical punishment. My mother was the disciplinarian. My seventh grade teacher was Mrs. Wiggins. I met her in my hometown years later when I was a middle school teacher, and she said that I was always angry. I remember being a little girl with no filters. I wonder why? I was always in trouble long before sixth and seventh grade.

I was born on Nicholson Street and lived there until I started first grade. One of the neighbors spoke to me; saying, "Hey Jannie," and I did not like his greeting. At the tender age of six, my mother taught me what would happen if I disrespected any adult. We had several fellowship groups over the years and certain religious gatherings had a spiritual and an educational component. One of the persons leading such group was a stern lady pastor named Elise Woodard. I do not remember my age at the time, but I do remember her telling one of the young ladies, "Jones, stay away from Jannie." I supposed that I was being disruptive or disrespectful. I was a little girl with a very strange personality.

Mother was no joke. She had lost an eye when she was a child and I fondly remember her being able to control all seven of her children from any angle of the room. All she had to do was to give you "The Look." Southern mothers often had large families. They were known for having complete control over their children, no matter how many they had. My mother was the primary disciplinarian. If you requested anything from my dad, he would send us to mother. My mother never allowed her disability to affect her life in a negative way.

Children were never left unattended, nor did we have organized daycare. We were cared for by our church affiliates most of the time.

Mother Cook was a senior woman who was an intricate part of our lives. She was a no-nonsense woman, typical for that era, and she was one of our caregivers. We would go to her house after school and probably during school vacations. There was a genuine sense of family. Mother Cook was a minister, who shared in ministry with her husband, Bishop Cook. They were pastors in Maple Shade in Portsmouth, Virginia, and they were affiliated with the Mount Calvary Holy Church, which played a major role in our lives as children and beyond. Outside of our regular church attendance, we were active in the Mount Calvary Junior Church. There were many benefits to the Mount Calvary connection. For instance, when I travelled anywhere that there was a Mount Calvary Church, I had an extended family.

Earlier I mentioned live-In jobs and relocating to the north. While in the Washington, D.C., area, I enjoyed a rich and warm fellowship with the Mount Calvary Church. I stayed in the bishop's home on my days off. The junior church also gave us the opportunity to learn about leadership in the church and lay the foundation for the leaders we have become today.

Our other caregiver was Sister Lucas. The Lucas family was a large family like ours. Sister Lucas was a widow and a stay-at-home mother. She was very strict and followed the

Bible to the letter. However, we enjoyed being with her children outside of church.

All I remember is childhood play. There was nothing like activities of today. Life was going to school, homework, and play. We had a lot of church. We could be in late night revival for weeks at a time and we still had to get up and be in school every day. Her oldest son, Joseph Lucas. became a preacher and we began to follow him when he would conduct revivals.

My Parents

My father, Deacon William A. Watson, Sr., was born on Eastern Shore, Virginia. Little is known of his early life, but he was a member of a large family. According to Dad, his father was a man who left a lot to be desired as a father. Dad shared with us some of the ways that his father was disrespectful to his mother and failed to provide adequately for the family, even though he had the means to do so. Dad, however, was an excellent father and a godly man, and because of him, we believe that a generational curse can be broken. Initially, he became a member of the AME Church and the Disciples of Christ. Later, when he met Bishop Jesse Handshaw, he became a member of Gospel Tabernacle, Cape Charles, Virginia. Dad was a very generous Christian, who gave his time and talent to the church and to mankind. He taught his children to do the same.

Once each month, Dad would travel from our home in Portsmouth to Cape Charles with Bishop Handshaw for service. Travel in those days, before the building of the

Chesapeake Bay Bridge in Virginia, was by ferry. Everything was church-centered, and "Thou Shalt Not" were the three words that dominated our lives. Everything was considered sin or sinful in the Holiness Church. Most activities, such as movies, were forbidden. We did not even ask to go. Today we freely participate in sports and other activities, such as acting, and achieve in those areas. In the early days, we did not wear any makeup and jewelry was limited to wedding rings. Of course, women did not wear pants and women would not go to church or any setting without pantyhose or stockings. There were so many unspoken rules and yes, many more unhappy children.

Mother, Cornelia Hansley Watson, was a native of Wilmington, North Carolina. Her mother died when she was seven years old, and she was raised by her father and step-mother. She was the oldest of seven siblings from her father's first marriage, and later he had ten children with his second wife. The last two of my grandfather's children were born the same year as my oldest sister and brother. Aunt Ernestine and my oldest sister, Bayne, were born in 1938. My brother, William Jr., and Uncle Rudolph were born in 1946.

Mother loved and cared for her siblings and they loved her in return. They affectionately called her Sister Nealie. They often shared stories of the nice things she did for them when they were growing up. Her life was rich because of her love for mankind. This was evident because of the many families with which she developed strong connections.

While living in Wilmington, Mother acquired an extended family that remained a loyal support team for her entire life.

The matriarch of the Boney family was Mama Louise, whose daughter, Isabel McGowan, was born the same year as Mother. We called her Aunt Pinksie, and she became the first school-teacher in the family. The Wilmington connection reached all the way to Portsmouth, Virginia, which my parents called home for the rest of their lives. In Virginia, my parents were well received by the Woodard Family and their relatives. We were always happy to see Uncle Percy and Aunt Letia Woodard, who lived in Pinners Point. Uncle Percy ran a small candy store and would frequently come bearing gifts and money. I am not sure when I discovered that they were not our biolog-ical family, because we were never treated differently. Aunt Letia was also a strong God-fearing woman who raised her five children in the fear and admonition of the Lord.

As a member of the Baptist Church, my mother proudly shared stories over the years of her strict training. She and my father met through mutual friends and they shared their strong religious beliefs. Her faith enabled her to instill strong Christian values in her children, and she was an inspiration to all persons she encountered. She was loved and respected by the families she worked for as a housekeeper. They were con-cerned about every aspect of her life. They often took care of our family needs, such as food and clothing. There was once a legal problem and a family for whom she worked helped her resolve it.

Mother was also a strong advocate of education. She was unable to attend school because of the death of her mother when she was very young, and she had to help with her younger siblings. Even though we grew up in the segregated South, my parents were strong examples of how living according to God's Word can make our lives richer. My mother was always involved in creative ways to make life better for her children. Three specific incidents come to my mind

1. There was a construction project near our home on Glasgow Street in Portsmouth, Virginia, in the 1940s. Mother would make a large pot of navy beans and apple jacks (apple turnovers) and sell lunch to the construction workers. I am sure that we needed the money to make ends meet.

2. When it was time for Marion to graduate in 1959, as usual, times were tight financially. Mother took a job as a short order cook at Alexander's Corner, which was located near our home. I wonder today just how she was able to adapt to a job such as that. She was an excellent cook, but she had always worked for private families.

3. Mother was sixty years old when she took a summer housekeeping job in Quogue, New York, which is on the eastern end of Long Island. Mother kept in touch with that family after her assignment was over.

Her strength gives me the courage to keep striving to reach my goals. She was an amazing woman.

We attended segregated schools all my life in the South. All my teachers were black. The only white people I saw were the itinerant music teacher and a band teacher. After we relocated to the outskirts of town, we rode a bus to school. We passed by several white-only schools along the way and our schools did not have the same resources as the schools for white students.

There were colored and white bathrooms, water fountains, no hotel accommodations and no restaurants. Segregation was degrading and demeaning. I also believe that it was conditioning. In other words, there was a certain behavior expected because of race, and in order not to become a troublemaker, we settled for life as it was. I never dreamed of the life that I enjoy today. No matter how smart or intelligent I was, life was hard because of my economic status. My family did not have the money or the information to allow me to go beyond high school.

Stores such as Woolworth's and Grants were popular in the South, and they are historical subjects today because of the "sit-ins" in the South for the purpose of integration. My sons only know about such subjects because of history. Blacks could go to a specific section to purchase food but could not sit at the counter to eat.

On February 1, 1960, four students from all-black North Carolina Agricultural and Technical College walked into a Woolworth five-and-dime with the intention of ordering lunch. But the manager of the Greensboro Woolworth's had intentions of his own — to maintain the lunch counter's strict whites-only policy.

Franklin McCain was one of the four young men who shoved history forward by refusing to budge. McCain remembers the anxiety he felt when he went to the store that Monday afternoon, the plan he and his friends had devised to launch their protest, and how he felt when he sat down on that stool.

"Fifteen seconds after ... I had the most wonderful feeling. I had a feeling of liberation, restored manhood. I had a natural high. And I truly felt almost invincible. Mind you, [I was] just sitting on a dumb stool and not having asked for service yet," McCain says.

"It's a feeling that I don't think that I'll ever be able to have again. It's the kind of thing that people pray for ... and wish for all their lives and never experience it. And I felt as though I wouldn't have been cheated out of life had that been the end of my life at that second or that moment."

McCain shares his recollection of the exchanges the four African-American men had with the lunch-counter staff, the store manager and a policeman who arrived on the scene — and also a lesson he learned that day.

An older white woman sat at the lunch counter a few stools down from McCain and his friends.

"And if you think Greensboro, N.C., 1960, a little old white lady who eyes you with that suspicious look ... she's not having very good thoughts about you nor what you're doing," McCain says.

Eventually, she finished her doughnut and coffee. And she walked behind McNeil and McCain — and put her hands on their shoulders.

"She said in a very calm voice, 'Boys, I am so proud of you. I only regret that you didn't do this ten years ago.'" McCain recalls. "What I learned from that little incident was ... don't you ever, ever stereotype anybody in this life until you at least experience them and have the opportunity to talk to them. I'm even more cognizant of that today— situation like that — and I'm always open to people who speak differently, who look differently, and who come from different places," he says.

On that first day, Feb. 1, the four men stayed at the lunch counter until closing. The next day, they came back with fifteen other students. By the third day, 300 joined in; later, 1,000.

The sit-ins spread to lunch counters across the country — and changed history.[5]

I was fortunate in February 2018 to attend a ceremony in Hempstead, New York, where a street renaming took place honoring Joseph McNeil, one of the Greensboro Four. Angevine Street is now Joseph McNeil Street. My brother, Reverend Cornelius Watson, resides on Angevine Street and my sister, Elder Audrey Watson, resides in the Greenwich Housing, which has an entrance on Angevine Street.

My Siblings

Bayne Elvenia Watson Waddler was the first child born to the godly couple, Deacon William A. Watson, Sr., and Mother Cornelia H. Watson, on October 28, 1938. She was a born leader who was bright, energetic, and multi-talented. She attended the Portsmouth Public Schools and Tidewater Community College. Her first job was in food services, but eventually, her passion took her to the health care profession, and she worked hard performing her duties well.

After engaging in a conversation with her, people feel empowered to conquer whatever obstacles they faced. It is no surprise that Bayne obtained a driver's license at the age of fifteen and became the family chauffeur as well as a driver for others. Her love of cars and driving led her into the transportation business, where she also excelled. Eventually, her son,

Brett, joined her, and they dominated their territory. This tireless lady, with a flair for clothing, would create suits, dresses, and accessories for anyone. Of course, one of her favorite pastimes was shopping, and she would also search for curtains and pillows to brighten up any room.

Church was the order of the day for the Watson family, and Bayne made her own personal commitment to Christ at a young age and became a loyal and dedicated servant. She was a member of New Covenant Church in Portsmouth for many years, but later joined the Garden of Prayer COGIC under the leadership of the late Bishop L.E. Willis Sr. She loved her church and was very active in the ministry. When she traveled from church to church with the family, she would create Bible trivia and adapt songs to suit the occasion. She was truly wise beyond her years and had the ability to cut through red tape and handle her business. Most of all, however, she had the gift of encouragement, even though there were times when she was in pain.

Marion Delorise Watson Bowers, the second child of Deacon William Watson Sr., and Mother Cornelia H. Watson, was born December 8, 1940. She was educated in the public-school system of Portsmouth, Virginia, and later she attended Norfolk State College in Norfolk, Virginia. She is a member of the Faith Temple Worship Center in Virginia Beach, Virginia. The most social of the Watson family, Marion is always busy planning something and moving around. She is a free spirit who loves to cook and fills her calendar with activities in Virginia and New York. We remember her as the family childcare person, a talented seamstress, an event planner, known as Sis Goodman and most of all, one who has never met a stranger. Marion acquired the nickname "Sis Goodman" because of a dear family friend who would come to visit periodically and literally take over our small, meager and inadequate household. She would have us cleaning up, and as I remember, she was strict. The lady's real name was Maggie Goodwin and she was also the person who introduced my parents to each other. As life unfolded, Marion was the family babysitter and all of the children tell stories of how strict she was.

Elder Audrey Olivia Watson, the fourth child of Deacon William Watson Sr., and Mother Cornelia H. Watson, was born on June 15, 1944 in Portsmouth, Virginia. She also began her education in the Portsmouth, Virginia public school system, but she attended Crestwood High School, when the family relocated to the outskirts of town. She enjoyed cheerleading, chorus, and gymnastics. She graduated from Crestwood in 1963.

Audrey became a faithful church member like her siblings, and at an early age joined the Evergreen Apostolic Faith Church of God Live On in Wilroy, Virginia, under the leadership of Elder Winfield Ridley. She attended all services and participated in many activities. After high school, she relocated to Hempstead, New York, where she was befriended by Rev. James Hallman, pastor of the Community Temple COGIC, and his family. Her life was filled with many activities, including working at E.J. Korvette Department Store, attending business school, and holding a variety of jobs. Eventually she joined the health care profession, where she enjoyed working as a personal care aide. One of her favorite activities was singing in a group formed by her childhood friends, Margaret Williams, Robert Ellis, and John Griffin.

Audrey is proud of her daughter, Lasetta, son-in-law, James Simeona, and three grandchildren, James IV, Shakinah, and Micah. In addition, she is the godmother of seven, and a surrogate mother to many others, including some nephews. Her commitment to mankind far exceeds her biological borders.

In 1989, Audrey joined the Saint John Baptist Church in Westbury, under the leadership of her brother, Rev. William A. Watson Jr. She immersed herself in the life of the church with her gifts and talent as a renowned gospel singer. God called her higher and she preached her initial sermon on April 14, 1996. As a very dedicated steward of the gospel, Audrey travels the East Coast attending conferences and preaching.

Reverend William A. Watson Jr. is the fifth of seven siblings and the first male child born to Deacon William A. Watson Sr., and Mother Cornelia H. Watson. Educated in Virginia's public-school systems, he relocated to Jamaica, New York, when he was eighteen years old. He later moved to Hempstead, New York, and continued his education at the Manpower Development Training School, New Hyde Park, New York.

William Albert Watson Jr. began his spiritual journey at the Living Sacrifice Church of God in Christ under the leadership of Elder Haward Webb in 1964. He often speaks of the valuable training that he received while he was chairman of the Trustee Board of Living Sacrifice. He later joined the Faith Baptist Church, where he was an usher, choir member, van driver, and attended Tuesday Night Bible study, taught by Reverend Constance Anderson. He continued to study the Word of God and to faithfully serve the Lord, and in 1978 responded to the call to the gospel ministry. He was licensed to preach in June of 1978 and ordained in July of 1979 as assistant to the late Rev. Joseph Howell. In January of 1983, he was called as interim pastor to the St. John's Baptist Church, Westbury, New York, and in April of 1983 was called as senior pastor of St. John's Baptist Church, where he has been the pastor for the past thirty-six years. In addition, he has served as pastor of the Free Will Baptist Church in Freeport, New York, since 2009.

Rev. Watson considers his responsibility is first and foremost to "bring souls to Christ." The St. John's Baptist Church edifice, constructed from the ground up, debt-free, is testament to the same. During his many years of ministering God's Word, he has birthed several new and valuable works in his churches. The list includes a prison evangelical program, a radio ministry, a hospital outreach program, and development and leadership training.

Rev. Watson's influence extends over the state and the country as he actively works with the National Baptist Convention, U.S.A. Inc.; Empire Baptist Missionary Convention, Inc., New York State; Eastern Baptist Association of New York, Inc.; and the Hampton Minister's Conference. As a self-employed, retired businessman, and a fifty-four-year resident of Hempstead, New York, he continues to be on the front line of the struggle for unity and the empowerment for the church and our people. He spends much of his time working with the Baptist Pastor's Conference in Hempstead and vicinity as chaplain for the Village of Hempstead's Police Department; chairperson of the Minority Affairs Council of Nassau County; president of the Long Island Conference of Clergy; and a member of the Black Jewish Coalition for Justice.

One of the proudest moments in the life of Rev. Watson occurred on July 17, 2003, when he was successfully elected as moderator of the Eastern Baptist Association of New York, Inc. He held this position for two terms. On October 2, 2005, the All Christian Bible College conferred upon him an honorary doctoral degree. On August 10, 2009, he received a certificate from Bishop Richard Cross Sr., declaring that he was also Elder William A. Watson Jr., from his home church El-Bethel Worship Center in Suffolk, Virginia. He received a Doctorate of Christian Education Certificate on July 18, 2015, and an Honorary Chaplain License certificate and badge on October 18, 2015, from the Anointed by God Ministries. We thank God for the successes of our brother and ask God for His continued blessings.

Reverend Cornelius Winfield Watson Sr. was born on March 12, 1952, in Portsmouth, Virginia. He was the second male in the Watson clan. He was a good student who was well-liked when he attended the local public schools. Nealie, as he is affectionately called by his siblings, was known for his musical talent and his ability to remember details. At the age of thirteen, he moved to New York with his older siblings where he first attended a junior high school in the Bronx and later attended Hempstead High School, in Hempstead, New

York. Through the years, he showed his love as he helped his family in many ways. After holding several jobs, he became a New York City traffic officer.

Rev. Annie Larine Watson Townsend was born on September 6, 1948, in Portsmouth, Virginia. She was the baby girl of the family, and we called her <u>Baby Ann.</u> She attended the local public schools where she demonstrated her skills and talent. Later she moved to Poughkeepsie, New York, then to Jamaica, New York, and attended their local schools. She was given the gift of song and taught herself to play the piano.

Annie joined the Zion Tabernacle Fire Baptized Church in Jamaica, New York, with her husband, Rev. Moses Townsend Jr. They later relocated to South Carolina, where Rev. Townsend served as a pastor in Marion and Georgetown, South Carolina. Annie also accepted the call to the ministry and organized the Christian Family Crusade. At one time, she also pastored a church in Rochester, New York. While serving a strong, dedicated group of followers, she was able to help many people. In addition, she earned a certificate at the Manpower Training Institute in New Hyde Park, New York, where she developed a love for senior care. This enabled her to work in the field of geriatric nursing. Finally, she loved to travel, and her employment allowed her to see the north, south, east, and west of our country.

Annie passed away in November 2003, leaving family and friends with a deep hurt and some large shoes to fill. However, her legacy and contributions to the church and to mankind will live on through her biological and adopted children and grandchildren. All of her children now reside in the Atlanta,

Georgia area. Her oldest daughter, Loretta Townsend Wilson, resides in Stockbridge, Georgia, with her husband, Percy Wilson Sr., who works for Delta Airlines; children, Tangela, who is a supervisor for the Marriott Hotel, and Percy Jr., who is employed by Avis Rental Car Service.

Annie's oldest son, Erik, resides in Riverdale, Georgia, with his wife, Autiki. Erik is employed by Southwest Airlines and Autiki drives an eighteen-wheeler. They are the parents of three daughters and one son. Daughter number one, Briannti, is a Marine and is married to a Marine, Quinton Reese. Daughter number two Eriqa, is December, a graduate of Tennessee State University. Daughter number three, Eryn, is a recent high school graduate from Munday Mills High School, Riverdale, Georgia and also received her associate's degree from Georgia State Military Academy.

Warren Jermaine is Annie's third child. He is a bus driver and resides in Riverdale, Georgia, with his wife, Lisa, who is a social worker.

During her travels with her husband and her own ministry, Annie met many people. One of the most interesting people was a young lady nicknamed "Virl," later known as Colonel Virvitine Sharpe. Recently, while on a cruise to the Bahamas, Virl shared with me that Annie took her on her first plane ride when she was about twelve years old. Virl was a member of the Fire Baptized Church in Georgetown, South Carolina, and became the family babysitter. Virl graduated high school in South Carolina and entered the United States Army. She was on active duty and worked for the Dept. of Corrections in Virginia while also in the reserves. After the closing of the correctional facility in Lorton, Virginia, she returned to active duty and rose to the rank of colonel. Virl is married to veteran Robb Sharpe. They are the parents of two children, and they reside in Birmingham, Alabama.

Chapter 2

SEARCH FOR BETTER OPPORTUNITIES

After high school, I moved around a great deal, seeking employment. Much of my time was spent in the Washington, D.C., area; specifically Rockville and Silver Spring, Maryland, where sleep-in jobs were available. Northern employment agencies would place advertisements in southern newspapers for live-in (sleep-in) domestic workers. All transportation, room and board were provided until the worker was placed with a family. The maid would take over all the housekeeping duties, cooking, and childcare. Most families considered all aspects of the lives of their help and were very generous to the help. Over the years, the hired help would be treated as family. Families would assist with gifts, loans, and influence when necessary. The work was not easy, but I learned so much about money management and banking from my employers and living in another kind of structured family.

While there, I connected with the Mount Calvary Holy Church under the leadership of Bishop Brumfield Johnson. In Virginia, I had attended the Mount Calvary Holy Church in an area called Maple Shade, where Bishop and Mother Cook were the leaders. I became a member of the "Junior Church" of the Mount Calvary Movement. That association opened many doors for me in years to come. I was so pleased to live with Mother Johnson in Washington, D.C., and attended the local Mount Calvary Church. Church was always the center of my life.

Migration to New York

In the summer of 1963, my life changed forever. My last sleep-in job was in Connecticut. The nature of those jobs allowed a person to establish a life in the community. Therefore, I was able to spend a short, but meaningful time with a small congregation where my associations reached back to my roots in Virginia.

My sister Audrey was living and working on Long Island, New York, and we both ended up at home in Virginia at the end of the summer. We agreed that we would settle together, whether in New York or Connecticut. Audrey had come to New York earlier with her god-sister, Margaret Ann Williams, who was a musically talented lady from a God-fearing family. Ann met Rev. James Hallman, pastor of Community Temple Church of God in Christ. We were invited to live with the Hallman family, and we roomed with them for about six months. Rev. Hallman later became my lifelong mentor and educational advisor.

It is now 2018, and we have been in New York since 1963. We must believe in divine destiny.

We were known as a church family in the South. When we relocated, we connected with the church. There are four of us in Nassau County. All of us are ordained Baptist ministers and we are very active in all areas of ministry and community activities. We are called upon in emergency situations. My brother, Rev. William A. Watson Jr., is the pastor of two churches: Saint John Baptist Church of Westbury, New York, and Free Will Baptist Church of Freeport, New York. He led the Saint John Baptist Church into a new edifice, constructed from the ground up, in 1997, debt-free. He is the former Moderator of the Eastern Baptist Association. In August 2018, Pastor William A. Watson Jr., was consecrated Bishop in the Apostolic Faith Church of God Live On in Suffolk, Virginia. This is the movement that we grew up in and our parents were founding members. On November 30, 2018, Bishop Richard H. Cross Sr., and his official staff convened at Saint John Baptist Church in Westbury, New York to install Bishop William A. Watson Jr., as leader of the Northern Diocese of the AFCOGLO.

Audrey is the founder of Healing Hurting Women, a group designed to help women facing difficult times and issues. I am the founder of Dorcas Outreach Ministries, designed to assist persons with day-to-day basic needs. Today all of us and our children are involved in ministry.

My Village

The Kennedy family was my first employer in New York, and they became a significant force in my life. Because I was familiar with domestic work, I practically ran their home for sixteen years. They lived on Kensington Road, Garden City, New York, when I first went to work for them in the fall of 1963. Later, they moved to Whitehall Boulevard. This began a life-long association, and I began to call them "My other family." Mr. Kennedy was a stockbroker, and Mrs. Kennedy was a busy homemaker who was very active with Catholic Charities. Betsy was ten and John Jr., fifteen at that time.

During my years of employment, my quality of life was greatly enhanced because the Kennedy family was always concerned about my life as a whole, and they helped me in many ways. In 1972, I obtained my driver's license, and when I informed Mrs. Kennedy that I wanted a car, she made it possible for me to purchase a brand new 1973 Malibu Chevrolet and allowed me to set the terms to pay for it. After graduating from college in 1978, I wanted to buy a house. Again, the favor of God was on my life. I found the house that is still my home, a house in Roosevelt, for which I could assume the owner's mortgage for a reasonable down payment. When I called Mrs. Kennedy to explain that I had been looking for a house, my sentence was interrupted with the question, "What do you need?" Another question was, "When can you go to Albany to help Betsy, who is now married and a mother?" Of course, my response was, "Immediately." In October 1979, I moved into my new home. My family has enjoyed so many privileges because of the generosity of the Kennedy family. I will always be grateful to God for His many blessings to me and for the persons He used to bless me. The Kennedy family has always been there for me and my family.

For the next fifteen-plus years, I worked in several areas before attending college: housekeeper, childcare and private dinner parties. My primary area was Garden City.

My first friend in New York was Malinda Sawyer. She lived in the neighborhood near Rev. Hallman, and she reached out to me. We shared a lifelong bond until her death. Our paths always crossed, and nothing was ever more devastating to me than her death. Her granddaughter, who was a student in the Roosevelt Middle School, walked into my office, burst into tears, and told me that her grandmother had died. My mind went back to the days when we walked the streets of Hempstead, sharing in good and bad times. We were always there for each other, and she was also the godmother of my second son, Wayne.

One person who holds the record for being one of my longest friends in New York is Elder Haward Webb. Loyalty and dedication are the words that come to mind when I think of this gentleman's relationship to the Watson family. This serious, kind, very generous pastor of the Living Sacrifice COGIC Church always had words of encouragement and support when I was going through one of the lowest points in my life. His no-nonsense policy forced me to face reality, to get a grip on life, and to keep moving. He has remained loyal and dedicated and is always there for our family. I met

Elder Webb in 1963. He was my husband's pastor. My brother William was also a member of Pastor Webb's ministry.

While serving in that ministry, according to the tradition of the times, I acknowledged my call to ministry in February 1965. During those years, we were recognized as "Inspired Missionaries." The Senior Missionaries would invite the new/young missionaries to participate on "Platform Services," and give us five minutes to tell our story. The experience was great and training was priceless.

Meeting Mr. West

In November 1963, the day of President John Kennedy's funeral, Mr. Eartley West Sr., and I crossed paths. After a whirlwind courtship, we were married on May 16, 1964, in my little country church in Wilroy, Virginia. My mother prepared a reception in our home in Portsmouth, Virginia. My very handsome, dark-complexioned groom of medium height and I set off to begin a life of marital bliss.

Mr. West was smart and a talented guitar player. He was called to the ministry and preached his initial sermon in 1965. During our marriage, he held several jobs. He was employed by the Long Island Railroad until he became a data entry operator for Stern's Department Store. After the birth of our son, Allen, he returned to the Veteran's Administration and assumed the position he had previously held in his early years in New York. Eventually, he moved to the hospital security position, which he held until he retired.

Marriage was intermittent and bittersweet. More bitter than sweet. Over the years, I realized that our early lives shape or determine our future outcome. Eartley West Sr. lost his father at age fifteen. I do not pretend to be a psychologist or a person to diagnose any problems, but since I was the recipient of his undesirable behavior, I will draw a conclusion. He never dealt with the loss of his father, and as the saying goes, "Hurt people hurt people." He was in and out of our lives until 1982, when Allen was two years old. Remember, he left when I was pregnant with Harold in 1970. He was missing most of the time for the next eight years. When he returned in 1978, I was ready to graduate from college.

After the dissolution of the marriage, we civilly co-parented until his death in 2007.

Motherhood

One of the most gratifying feelings was to become a mother, and I am still fascinated with motherhood. Boys were to become my biological heritage. Eartley Jr., was born on February 18, 1965. As a much-disciplined person, he became a role model and raised the bar high for his brothers and cousins. One of my greatest joys has been to watch my sons and other males in our family become nurturing and committed fathers. Eartley Jr., became a father at age twenty-one in 1986, while he was in the Marines, and the mother of his daughter was also a Marine. His daughter, Sarah, is now thirty-two years old and is the mother of a seven-year-old son.

After the Marines, Eartley Jr. worked for the U. S. Postal Service while also trying to break into the acting field and also building a singing career. Presently, he sings with the East Coast Band of Long Island and he is a Real Estate Broker. He performs for weddings and some church events. His Gift of song took him to Cuba while singing with his church choir.

Wayne Albert was born on May 30, 1966, and he became a quiet "me too" kid. However, his self-expression was realized when he was promoted during Marine basic training. As a child, Wayne seemed to always be dependent and never really showed interest in anything. He did not care too much for school and therefore he was just an average student. Wayne left New York in 1986 and after leaving the Marines he made Charlotte North Carolina his home. In Charlotte, Wayne has a new family. While in the Marines, Wayne met Sydney Phillips, whom he embraced as his brother and Sydney Mother as his other mother who he affectionately refers to as Mama Kay. Wayne became a father in 2001. His daughter, Jasmine, is a special needs child. Wayne has raised her as a single parent. He has been a devoted parent and has been diligent concerning her education. Her present abilities far exceed the limits of her diagnosis of <u>Williams Syndrome.</u> Jasmine graduated from high school in 2019, and was being prepared for a life skills program. Wayne is also the godfather of many other young people.

Harold Cornelius was born on August 25, 1970 and is now a founder of a church in Schenectady, New York, with his wife and co-pastor, Saretha. They are parents of three biological children: Harold, Jr., a newlywed (wife Alayna), Ahteras, and Lynn. Harold Jr. and Ahteras are licensed ministers.

Life had thrown me a curve ball when Harold was born. It was a time of loneliness, despair, and desolation, but I did not have time to wallow in sorrow. I had two little boys and another one on the way. I should have had a good cry or emotional expression, but I held it together in public. However, inside I was hurting. The children never saw me out of control or moping around. I stayed busy with work, church, and raising my family. All during this time, I was helping other family members and my parents. Work is therapeutic.

My anchor was in God, who kept me focused. It is possible to survive the misfortunes of life. Surround yourself with people. Stay faithful in prayer, service, and outreach. Worship your way through. Sarah did not give up on God. Even though she was unhappy because she had not given her husband a male child, she continued to worship.

What the enemy meant for my demise, God turned completely around and showed me His divine favor, and all aspects of my life were blessed. Harold's birth ushered a prosperous component into my life, and everything I touched turned to gold. So many wonderful things have since occurred, as I mentioned earlier in this book. I attended college and obtained my degree. I became a teacher and later an assistant principal. I was also ordained as a Baptist minister in 1990, and later

in 1991, I founded the Dorcas Outreach Ministries and along with a faithful group of supporters, we help others to secure food, clothing, and household items and in any other way that we can. We can be called on a very short notice and there is no red tape to cut through.

On April 29, 2012, I was invited to preach at the Deeper Life Fellowship and Deliverance Center in Schenectady, New York. Later, the name was changed to the Greater Faith Ministries and I am proud to announce that Pastors Harold and Saretha Johnson West are now leading that thriving congregation. I learned from my life experiences that we are blessed to be a blessing.

They have recently purchased a church building with a parsonage with two large parking lots. Their ministry is growing and includes outreach ministries which include a food pantry and other family services.

Blessing number four, Allen Lyron, was my midlife surprise, Allen Lyron, and the other three children are my heartbeats. They gave me a reason to set my goals high and to work hard to be successful. His brothers, other family members and my girlfriends, (All mothers of adult children), welcomed my new bundle of sunshine. Eartley, Jr. was so happy, he would come and get Allen in the morning while he was getting dressed for school. Junior said, "I cannot wait until he is old enough to stay in my room." That never happened, because after high school, Eartley Jr., joined the Marines. Harold was ten years old when Allen was born. He asked me to teach him how to change his diaper. At the tender age of ten, Harold was my best babysitter. Of course, Lisa (Lasetta), My niece, was Allen's second mother.

Allen's life was a challenge because he was born legally blind. He wore thick glasses and he was in special education until sixth grade because of his vision. Allen went to Roosevelt Middle School and was an honor student. Later, he became restless after his brothers left home and moved to Virginia and Georgia. He returned to New York, passed the GED Test and marched with his class in 1999.

On August 31, 2018, Allen married the lovely Nicole Jackson, aka "Queen Nikki." The family is overjoyed with the new addition to our family. Queen Nikki is a bright, gifted and focused young lady. Her family was connected with our family through the church. Nikki is an elder in the New Beginnings Worship Center in Bellmore under the leadership of Apostle Althea Jackson. The Royal West Wedding was one of three highlights of the family in August 2019. The other two were 1. August 4. 2019 was the wedding of my oldest grandson, Harold West, Jr., and Alayna in Schenectady, New York. 2. The consecration of my brother, Reverend William A. Watson, Jr. as Bishop.

Many moments in my life were like the laughter that Sarah felt when she heard that she was going to have a baby in her senior years. Such is the case with Harold and Allen. Both faced educational challenges, but today Harold is just a part of my success story. Allen now works as a lab technician and with the aid of medical science, has normal eyesight and is an all-around great son. I am proud to be the mother of four by birth, but many others by association. Later in Sarah's story, Sarah said that God had made her to laugh and all that heard her story would laugh with her.

The African American tradition and culture is to share parenting responsibilities among family members, should the need arise. Many times, over the years, it was necessary to care for nieces, nephews, and others. My home was always open to others. Lasetta (Lisa) Watson, the daughter of my sister Audrey, lived with me during her childhood years. Audrey and I came to New York in 1963 and we lived together most of the time. When Audrey was away or working, Lisa was my girl. Some people refused to believe that I was not her mother. What a difference a girl makes in a household.

Lisa (Lasetta) was a busy, energetic young lady. She is a teacher, talented singer, and a minister. She is the proud mother of three children: James IV, Shakinah Mone', and Micah. James is a security guard and Micah is a college student. Again, girls bring much energy to the table. Shakinah is a bright, talented young lady. She was an honor student throughout her life. She excelled in college and went to China as an exchange student during her last year in college.

Psalm 34 King James Version (KJV) 34:1 *I will bless the* LORD *at all times: his praise shall continually be in my mouth.*[6]

This is the scripture that sustained me through my trying times and continues to keep me grounded. Life has dealt me some severe blows, but because of my strict religious upbringing, I believe the Word of God unconditionally. The pain is the same as it is for everyone else, but I know that despite what it looks like, God loves me.

Harold and Allen had a special needs diagnosis, and in both cases I had to fight for services for them. As I pursued higher education, other educators would express surprise that I was so transparent about the needs of my children. I realized that it was my duty to give my boys the best that I had. I did not want them to be twenty-one years old and unable to provide for themselves because of my pride. Today, I am the proud mother of two fine men who are great husbands and fathers. Allen came out of the system and was an honor student. Harold and his wife are founders and pastors.

I learned so much as I worked my way through the system. I also obtained a master's degree in special education along the way. I have been able to help many students and families because of my own personal experiences.

Many parents' first reaction when they realize that their child has needs outside of the norm is to blame themselves or to be in denial. Both reactions are a disservice to the child. As a parent, you should seek help for the child as soon as you are made aware that there is a problem. The classroom teacher's hands are tied if the parent is in denial, and unfortunately, most parents' first reaction is denial. Children become frustrated when they are unable to perform academically, and it sometimes causes a child's behavior to become a problem. I had no idea that a career in education would become the blessing that keeps on giving, and I am so grateful when I can share my personal story and help others.

In addition to my biological children, nieces and nephews, there are others who captured my heart. I am a nurturer by nature. Durwood Cox Jr., and his brother, Demon, came into my life when they were about seven and eight years old. Demon is Allen's age and they spent a lot of time in my home. The three boys also spent the summers in Rochester, New York, with my youngest sister, Rev. Annie Townsend, who had an outreach ministry. While in Rochester, Annie would assign them positions in the church. Rev. Townsend was strict, but the boys enjoyed their time with her and their cousins and other extended family. After Durwood graduated from Hempstead High School, in Hempstead, New York, he worked in food services in Roosevelt District where I was employed. He worked in a few of the five schools in the district. His main school was Ulysses Byas.

True Story:

One day his mother, Beverly Cox, went to the school looking for him. She asked for Durwood Cox and was told that there was no one there by that name. However, there was a Mr. Durwood West who worked there. The staff really believed that he was my biological son. When they called Mr. West, he answered. He did not correct them. He is a true son, and everyone knows that he is one of my favorites. Durwood fathered a son when he was teenager. He immediately accepted his responsibility and tried to provide for his son. When Durwood III was about a year old, Durwood called to ask me if he could do something for me to earn money to buy his son a birthday gift. I am the go-to person in the family when anyone needs something. He came to my house at that time and remained until he got married.

True Story:

One of the traditions of the African American church is that when you join the church, you automatically become family. It is very common for young people to walk up to the elders and call them mommy, auntie, or some other endearing term, even grandma. So technically everyone in church is related, and as the pastor's family, we are kin to everybody. Years ago, early in ministry, I was going to minister in Long

Beach and I asked my nieces to go with me: Lisa, Pam and Sheryl. They were about twelve and thirteen years old. During the service, they were on their knees praying and they started to speak in tongues. They were really into the praying and they were really, I mean they were *really* going in. I said to myself then, "They will have to live another whole lifetime to catch it with their testimonies." The three young ladies were behaving as though they were much older and had more experience. Today they are wonderful mother and I am proud of them. I was concerned at the time that they could face some pitfalls if you miss any part of life's lessons. I wanted them to slow down and live. Over the years when I told the story, it was funny, and we laughed about it. Sheryl is now a member of the Saint John Baptist Church. As a matter of fact, she is the choir director, and whenever I want a good laugh I just say to Sheryl, "I'm going to tell your story," and she says, "Please, Aunt Jannie, do not tell that story."

Life in the Church of God

My family later joined the Church of God in Jamaica, New York, under the leadership of Bishop Charles Allen. I continued to serve in ministry and became licensed as an evangelist. I organized an ecumenical group, The Northern District Fellowship Group. Pastors from all segments of the Pentecostal and the Baptist churches primarily joined us. Some of the pioneers were Bishop John Freeman Sr., Bishop John Freeman Jr., Bishop Charles Sessions, Rev. Joseph Howell, Elder Jerry Woods, and others. We traveled all over wherever ministry called us. In 1990, I was ordained as a Baptist minister along with seven other women. It was a history-making occasion, because the question of women in ministry is not settled in the Baptist denomination. Presently, I serve as assistant to Bishop Watson.

My passion is to help others to reach their full potential. I was given a second chance to live an abundant life, and there was a time when I did not have much hope. Earlier, I mentioned Bishop Allen, pastor of the Church of God, and Bishop Freeman, pastor and founder of the First Corinthians Church, Bronx, New York. Their churches supported me through the darkest hours in my life. Today and for the rest of my life, my goal is to give back in any way that I can; time talent and resources...

Life is about making a difference and daily I reflect on the scripture:

Psalm 116:12 *What shall I render unto the LORD [for] all his benefits toward me?*

And my favorite quotes:

"An obstacle is what you see when you take your eye off of your goal." Author Unknown

Chapter3

BLESSINGS AND UNCOMMON FAVOR

H ead Start (childcare) and the Arthur O. Eve Higher
Education Opportunity Program (HEOP) (college funding).

Head Start[7]

H ead Start was a childcare program operated under the
auspices of the local Community Action Program
(CAP). The program was very comprehensive; it included
breakfast and lunch and was free to qualified recipients. It
required active parent participation. There were so many com-
ponents to the program. One specific piece was health care.
The guidelines were very strict, and to maintain your place in
the program everything had to be followed to the letter.

Higher Education Opportunity Program

My life is filled with situations outside of the norm. It is evident now that I had the aptitude to obtain a college education. However, due to my family's economic status, it did not seem possible to me. I am not sure why the opportunities were so limited in the South.

In the North, when I had limited resources and a whole lot of responsibilities, fate stepped in. Not only did I attend college, but my program was fully funded. If someone had told me just a short time earlier that this was possible, I would have been like Sarah; I would have laughed. Even today, after seven years in retirement, I still pinch myself and say, "Thank You, God, for Your divine plan.

At thirty-two years of age, I began my quest for higher education and was fortunate to meet Sister Francis from Molloy College in Rockville Centre, New York. Sister Francis was my math teacher at the Education Opportunity Center, which was located on North Franklin Street in Hempstead, New York. She lived at the convent on the grounds of Molloy College. I lived near the borderline of Rockville Center, and Sister Francis needed a ride to the center. I became her chauffer. Consequently, she recommended me to Sister Regis Milhaven, director of the Higher Education Opportunity Program (HEOP).[8] my initial meeting was interesting because she told me that it was good that I had no money. Through her help, I was accepted into the program.

You cannot imagine how happy and proud I was to finally be enrolled at Molloy. During the four years at the college,

I received more than an academic education. Having been raised in the Pentecostal Church, I was not accustomed to the Catholic tradition of sharing with other religious groups. I sat daily with women of other races and bonded with them. Their concerns and needs were so different from those of the students in the HEOP program. For instance, I had a conversation with a young lady who was upset because she had no money of her own. (She had to rely on her husband for everything and she had to ask him for money any time that she needed something.) I met another young lady who was getting a divorce. Daily, I interacted with the other students and literally became a sounding board. I enjoyed all aspects of my years in college.

Because I was recruited by Sister Francis and she was my teacher during my first semester, she considered me to be a very good student and shared her feelings with her sisters and other faculty. I remember being in a new class and the teacher would call my name and say, "Oh, you're Jannie." Molloy was an all-female college but began to accept male students in the nursing program. When I count my blessings, I thank God first for my God-fearing parents, my life as a believer in Jesus Christ, my wonderful family, and for the day that I met Sister Francis Dominici from Molloy. My life and my destiny were changed forever.

In June 1978, I graduated with a bachelor's degree in sociology and a minor in elementary education. Molloy had been a real haven for me. I probably had a better appreciation than most, for this was a dream of mine that became an unimaginable reality. Today I realize that I was given a gift with an unlimited price tag, and that I must give back to a system that blessed me beyond my wildest dreams.

I am probably a professional student. The only reason that I did not stay in school is because I had the responsibility for my three sons. However, I knew that to solidify my career in education, I needed a master's degree. After inquiring about the master's program and receiving ads from CW Post, I enrolled in their master's program in September 1983, and completed my studies for a degree in special education in June 1985. Education was always on my mind, and I was never satisfied until I achieved my goals.

In 1988, I started to work toward an administrative certificate at the off-site campuses of Brooklyn College. When I was halfway through the program, when it was time for me to go to the main campus in Brooklyn, my application was rejected and I still am not sure why. It was probably because of enrollment quotas. I had to wait until the next semester and apply again. By that time, I was eager to complete that phase of my education. I decided to return to CW Post University, where I had completed my master's degree in 1985. I completed my courses in 1995. Almost immediately, I became the Director of Adult Education in my school district, and held that position for three years. I had been a teacher in the Adult Education Program for a number of years, and I enjoyed interacting with adult students. I was happy to share my story of going back to college as an adult. I really wanted to encourage them to reach for the sky.

Chapter 4

EDUCATIONAL CAREER

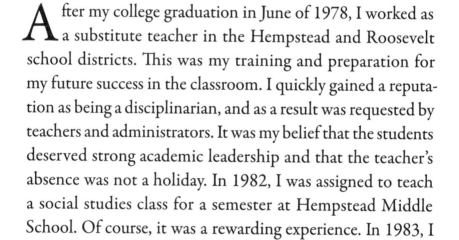

After my college graduation in June of 1978, I worked as a substitute teacher in the Hempstead and Roosevelt school districts. This was my training and preparation for my future success in the classroom. I quickly gained a reputation as being a disciplinarian, and as a result was requested by teachers and administrators. It was my belief that the students deserved strong academic leadership and that the teacher's absence was not a holiday. In 1982, I was assigned to teach a social studies class for a semester at Hempstead Middle School. Of course, it was a rewarding experience. In 1983, I returned to Roosevelt as a substitute and was hired as a junior high school social studies teacher in 1984. I remained as a teacher for fifteen years and was promoted to the position of assistant principal for the next five years.

This was an exciting journey, and I was good at it because I loved working with the junior high age group, and I was considered to be a strong disciplinarian. Very often, I was able to relate to known behavior problems. I was also able to get them to complete assignments. One of my greatest joys is to interact with former students who greet me; "Hi Miss West," I immediately know they are from my past in Roosevelt or Hempstead. Many times, students remember me, I recognize the faces, but cannot remember the name.

Life as a Teacher

The greatest joy in my secular life was to become a teacher. As a very young child and throughout my whole life, I kept the same dream. However, at some point, I thought that my dream would never come true. In June 1978, my dream came true when I graduated from Molloy College in Rockville, Centre, New York, with a bachelor's degree in sociology and New York State Certification, Nursery – Grade Six and Social Studies Grades seven through nine. I was on cloud nine.

The steps of a good man are ordered by the Lord.
Psalm 37:23

Finally, I began to see my dreams come true and my prayers were being answered daily. I begin my days watching "judge shows," and Judge Karen Mills-Frances says, "If you keep walking, you can turn your life around." It is my hope that as I share my story, your faith in God will be strengthened and your hope rekindled. Remember that sometimes the process is not always instant, and that is when patience is tested. Remember that Sarah was well past the childbearing age when the promise was fulfilled.

*Be not weary in well doing, we shall reap if we faint
not.* Galatians 6:9

It was my personal goal after college to become an elementary school teacher. I always tell the story of how I ended up in middle school. My degree in sociology gave me the extended Social Studies Seven through Nine New York State Certification. It was one of my many unexpected blessings.

Of course, I made some mistakes along the way. For example, I had difficulty completing my first report cards, but I quickly learned the process Also, I learned what battles to pick with the students. Many of the students came from immigrant parents who not only had education as a priority, but who were also strong disciplinarians. These ladies and gentlemen were my allies. Over the years, I developed warm and rich friendships and relationships. My students knew that I expected excellence, and as a result, I had a high promotion rate. I still meet students today who remind me that I was very strict.

Mrs. Luella Cohn, my first supervisor, was a great instructional leader. Although she was firm, she had a heart of gold. She taught me how to be a good teacher and prepared me well for tenure. It was a great day when she took me to the office of Dr. Phillip Smith, our principal, for my tenure interview.

Teaching on the 200 hall of the Roosevelt Jr – Sr High School was a pleasure. Some of the most rewarding relationships were formed during my fifteen years as a junior high social studies teacher. Jerri Smith, Elaine Voss, Stephanie Carlson, Bette Jane Houseman, and Suzanne Rupert were some of my fellow teachers. All of us are now Roosevelt retirees who attend monthly meetings and address specific information that relates to senior life.

I never imagined that my life would be enriched in the manner in which it was. While teaching, I had an opportunity to give back to a system that had provided me and my family with an abundant life. While I worked, I was not only able to provide for my family, I also gained much satisfaction from sharing with others. The staff members were a close-knit family and we worked together to meet the needs of our students. My neighborhood is considered in the lower socio-economic group, and some of the students live below the poverty level. Many of my students were in foster care and some were being raised by grandparents or other family members. The students adopted certain staff member and referred to them by endearing titles such as Auntie, Uncle, Godmother, Godfather, Grandmother and Mother or Mommy. We lived up to those titles, as we were often called upon to pool our resources to help students and their families. There were times that we would have requests from former students who were in college. Some staff members stepped into the role of parents and made financial provisions to allow students to be able to complete their college education.

Class Advisor

Class Advisor is a person appointed by the principal to move with a class until graduation. It is the duty of the advisor to lead the class in electing officers. The advisor solicits the help of parents and the school PTSA (Parent Teacher Student Association) to help with the fundraising activities and all events in regards to the specific class.

The advisor also plans for the senior trip. The class of 1990 was my first experience as an advisor. Mrs. Lillian Watson was my co-advisor and we took our class to Disneyland in Anaheim, California. It was a wonderful experience. Long, warm relationships were formed, and as always, I was adopted by some of the students.

My journey as advisor continued with the class of 1996. Again, the rewards continued and, as before, I was adopted by some of the students. I asked the staff to sponsor students so that they could go on the senior trip. The help and the response were overwhelming. In 1992, Najah Abdullah's (Class of 1996) entire family adopted me. We have remained close, and in 2015 I performed the wedding of Najah and Leo Smith.

Union Representative

Because of my strong, standup personality, I was drafted to become a union representative. This position kept me busy because there was always something out of compliance. David Carroll, a fine leader, trained us to protect the rights of the teachers. When he retired, he instructed us to follow the contract to the letter. I held this position for ten years until I became an administrator in 1999.

Adult Education Teacher/Director

I taught adult education for several years and the same year that I received my administrative certification, the adult education director retired. I spent three years as director. To be a part of adult education is an extremely rewarding experience. I enjoyed sharing with the students that I started college when I was 32 years old.

Assistant Principal

When the Roosevelt Jr. High School transitioned to Middle School Model, I was hired as the assistant principal. I had five wonderful years before being transferred to Pre K.

Although I am constantly reminded of my successful career while working in the Roosevelt School District, I did encounter a major problem with Central Administration in later years. However, it was not my intention to be disrespectful, and I do not feel the need to go into detail or spend a lot of time on this subject. The attack occurred when the district tried to deny me tenure as an administrator. I had literally carried the Roosevelt Middle School since its inception in 1999. They hired a principal who did not come during the first month of school in the 2000-2001 school years. The Department of Education in Albany had worked closely with us, and my name was a familiar one on the state level. Fortunately, the representative from the union interceded on my behalf, and I was given a fourth year. At the end of the year, I was invited to a meeting of the school board to be congratulated in-person for receiving tenure by the president of the school board. I refused to be bitter; I chose to keep my eyes on my goal and to continue to see the Big Picture,

Pre-Kindergarten

In 2004, after twenty years in the middle school, a new superintendent, Ronald Ross, assigned me as director of pre-kindergarten. I left the meeting highly upset because I did not realize that what I saw as a setback was a setup for a comeback. Five years of almost complete ecstasy is the way I remember and describe those years as pre-kindergarten director. They were exciting, interesting, and fun-filled, and I will always remember them as the most productive years of my life. The seasoned staff welcomed me with open arms. Catherine [Gladys Jackson] was the only person on the staff who was already my friend, and she actually came to the middle school with her friend, Laverta Cooks, to personally welcome me.

Pre-kindergarten was an oasis in the dessert, compared to my previous location. Eight buildings housed the program, which included so many perks. There were eight classrooms with an abundance of supplies. The reception building included a housekeeping area with a fully furnished kitchen and a laundry area. There were also all kinds of technology and other gadgets. The program consisted of eight teachers and eight teacher aides. Many staff members had longevity, and this created a real family-type setting.

There were three ladies whose efforts greatly helped us make the program a success. The first was my secretary, Anne Kallenberg. She was most efficient and handled all of the business in a timely manner. Every deadline was met because of her expertise. She had served the previous directors and knew how to guide me in my new position. The other two ladies were Karen Massenburg and Ramona Lipka. They were lead teachers who coached me during my entire tenure as director of the Roosevelt Pre-Kindergarten Center. These ladies will forever remain in my heart, and I shall always be indebted to them.

Although we continued to have a successful program, we faced some challenges as decisions were made to relocate us. We were first moved to the newly completed area of the Centennial Avenue School, where we stayed for one school year. Our next move was to the Harry Daniels Building, which was known as the little round school. We remained there for only one year. The next and final move was to the newly completed Washington-Rose School. The co-existence with Dr. Perletter Wright was a rewarding experience. She was a kind, compassionate, beloved educator. The two schools were a real family and we share wonderful memories, such as both staffs having celebrations together and our young ones being invited to assembly programs.

At the end of the second year, the program as we knew it was disbanded, and the students were placed in classrooms at the three elementary schools. I remember kindly the five pre-kindergarten years and the great relationships formed with the staff, parents and students. As life unfolds, it was my honor to be asked to present scholarships to the class of 2018 of the Roosevelt High School from the Roosevelt Retirees Organization. The students were a part of my first year as director of pre-kindergarten.

In September 2009, I was reassigned as assistant principal at the middle school. I dreaded returning to the middle school because I had begun to have mobility problems. I made all of the necessary arrangements to retire and the district was willing to allow me to retire with all of the benefits even without the traditional notice. After working three days, I changed my mind and decided to stay and I worked for two more years. Middle school students need special attention. They require strict rules, guidelines, and discipline. As stated earlier, over the years I became known as a "disciplinarian." However, it was also known that I could use behavior modification instead of harsh tactics. Loud reprimands were never a part of my discipline. I was also able to develop a warm and lasting relationship with the staff. I do not like to be referred to as the "Boss," I rather think of the staff as a team, and over the years, my philosophy worked well for me.

Chapter 5

SECOND MARRIAGE

The New Mays Family

February 2002, one of my teaching assistants, Kim Finney, who was like a daughter to me and always looked out for me, invited me to dinner. Larry Mays was one of the guests. We exchanged e-mail addresses and that was the beginning of an unlikely friendship. We had an Internet relationship, and eventually he asked me to meet his family. At that point, I realized that he was serious.

Larry is a retired bricklayer and a charter member of the Hempstead Gomillion Campbell American Legion Post. He is also a member of the 40 & 8, an Honor Society of the American Legion. His hobbies are golf and bowling. He loves to walk and to do his exercises. He is very health conscious. He spends his leisure time in his man cave watching sports and on his Kindle. He is an avid reader who reads the daily newspaper from cover to cover. When I met his family, I discovered that his sister and I had a lot in common. Not only is she an elder, but an active member of her church and a retired principal.

Since our storybook marriage on April 19, 2003, we have developed many positive relationships. Larry's brother, Warren, and his wife, Elder Naomi Mays (both now deceased), and my brother, Bishop William A. Watson, were a part of the Eastern Baptist Association. We visited Jacksonville, Florida, on two occasions, and the hospitality and love of the family was noteworthy. One of the most significant events in the family was the reunion of Larry and his grandson, Javon Julye, in Los Angeles. Larry is a great great grandfather

Love Beyond the Watson/Hansley Borders

When I began to think about this chapter, I became very emotional because I realized how important my extended family is to me. My mother was from a large family, the Hansleys in Wilmington, North Carolina, and my dad was also from a large family in Eastern Shore, Virginia. When I became a mother fifty-four years ago, I thought I knew what love was. I am sure that today that it was impossible for me to believe I could be loved by others and by other young people the same way that my children love me today.

I was excited every time I took on a new assignment, when I would go into a new building. Of course, I worked all over the Roosevelt Union Free School District, and I have had many assignments. I began my assignment in Roosevelt as substitute teacher in 1979. As I moved around the school world and the church world, young people would just automatically move toward me and some of them were my children's friends and some of them were my students and teachers on my staff. They started to claim me, to my surprise, and called me different titles: Auntie, Mommy, God-mommy, and I just loved it. Every time I had a new addition, I felt blessed.

Of course, I come from a large family of seven people. I had six brothers and four sisters. My oldest sister and my youngest sister have passed away. I have two surviving sisters and two brothers. I have my extended family, which reaches far beyond my wildest imagination. I'm just so excited about what is going on in my life, and as I sat down to write this, I was thinking about what I needed to say to the people who have befriended me and adopted me.

I just appreciate the love that you have shown me. I just want you to know I'm grateful to have you in my life. However, I am very afraid that I am going to miss someone in this process, and I do apologize if your name is not here. It's not because I don't love you, but it's because the human part of me cannot remember everything, and when you are my age you just can't remember everything that you need to. I am so excited about what God is doing in my life.

My extended borders are too numerous to include them all, but to me some of them are noteworthy. As previously stated, I was a junior high school social studies teacher. I had some wonderful students, and some of them stand out in my mind. One of my most recent stories is about a very bright student by the name of LaChrista Mann. I just might be guilty of showing favoritism, because I remember LaChrista fondly.

She was always prepared and she stood out in my mind over the years as I thought about her.

I believe that God has a sense of humor. Ten years ago, my biological brother, Bishop William A. Watson Jr., who is also my pastor, at the Saint John Baptist Church of Westbury, New York, became the pastor of a second church, Free Will Baptist Church of Freeport, New York. It was my pleasure to reconnect with one of my favorite students, LaChrista Mann Brown. She is now married to Reverend Curtis Brown, and they are the parents of three children. LaChrista is also a minister and I was privileged to sit on the examination for her ordination. Today, thirty years later, we are serving together in ministry and I am excited.

The story continues as I share the good news about those persons who have enriched my life. "You are my mother now," were the words spoken to me by Annie Cowans, following the death of her mother, Carrie Cowans. Annie is my new daughter, but her daughter, LaChrista, was my student thirty years ago.

Very often, I am greeted, "Hello, Mother," sometimes by persons who I did not know that they felt a kindred spirit to me. That was not the case with Karen Massenburg, a pre-kindergarten teacher at Bauer Avenue. There was an immediate connection between us. We had a common church interest. Karen became a part of my whole family. She was a young lady who had overcome some obstacles in life. I was sent to be the director of pre-kindergarten by the new superintendent, Ronald Ross. I was not happy; my entire career had been in middle school. Karen was one of the people who made my job easy. We bonded like glue. During my first year, she obtained her administrative certification and later began to work on her doctoral degree. We have a great mother-daughter relationship.

My life is filled with precious memories because of encounters beyond the family borders. When I moved to Roosevelt in 1979, I became "Aunt Jannie," to the entire Free and Independent Church Congregation on Debevoise Avenue, and the same is true today.

<u>True story:</u>

I was a substitute teacher for about six years after I graduated from college in 1978. I was assigned a class (supposedly a tough class) and when the teacher returned and asked about the behavior, she was sure that they gave me a hard time. She was shocked when I did not have any problems with the class. The secret was I was the aunt of the ringleader and he did not display his usual behavior with me. I have many stories over the years in which the outcome was the same. My experience as a substitute teacher prepared me for my success as a classroom teacher. I developed many techniques in order to motivate students. I was known as a no-nonsense teacher, and consequently I had a very high promotion rate.

...

Godmother

<u>Elder Helen Johnson,</u> Pastor, Faith Temple Worship Center, Virginia Beach, Virginia. Mother, as we call her, is the wife of the late Elder Robert Johnson. After his death, she assumed the pastoral duties of the church. We have been connected with this family for over fifty years. They have been there for us through thick and thin. My love for them goes back many years. I was visiting my parents in Portsmouth, Virginia, and I remember them as a very young couple painting my parents' home. Such kind acts have continued over the years, and after the death of our mother in 2004, Mother Johnson proudly claimed us as her children. She has shown us unconditional love. Our feelings are mutual toward her.

Sisters from another mother

<u>Apostle Jessie Edrington</u>
Founder and Overseer, Greater Temple of Blessings, West Hempstead, New York. (Gilliam, Calderon, Trollinger)
"Sister, Sister," is my greeting when I speak to this lady on the phone. Her family is among the first friends that I can recall meeting when I arrived in New York in 1963. Her mother, Mother Annie Gilliam, adopted our family as her own. A warm and wonderful relationship began and it continues to the present time. There is nothing that we do in ministry or in the secular that she is not a part of. Unconditional commitment is my best description of her.

Overseer Regina V. Johnson
Deeper Life Deliverance Center, Westbury, New York,
First sister friends for life, later family, "Gina" is what I call
her. Others call her "Reg." Loyalty, dedication, commitment are all terms that come to mind when I think of my
sister. She really knows how to get the job done and she
will never give up until it is done. She has weathered many
storms and has run interference for others. Before she became
a pastor, she served faithfully under the leadership of the
late Reverend Joseph J. Howell, pastor of the Faith Baptist
Church, Hempstead, New York, and for eight years she served
as assistant to Bishop William A. Watson Jr., pastor of the
Saint John Baptist Church, Westbury, New York. She is a
pastor, preacher, teacher and recently a published author of
book entitled, *The Missing Link*.

Lady Diane Deans
First Lady, Bethlehem of Judea, Hempstead, New York. Lady
Di, as we fondly refer to her, shares a special bond with us
through the "Old Pentecostal Church." I examine her clothes
to make sure that they are up to standards (private joke). We
share stories. She is our sister who helped us get through the
loss of the youngest Watson Girl, Reverend Annie Watson
Townsend. We love and appreciate her. She is the wife of our
brother, Pastor Lynwood Earl Deans. This Dynamic Duo has
stood with our family for over forty years.

Jerrie Smith, aka Sugar, Co-worker

"Sugar" is what we call her. She loves everybody. I have only seen her angry one time in our forty-year friendship. She is one of my most reliable and dedicated friends in the whole, wide world. She is the only person who has ever celebrated my birthday in October, when I was born in August. You have to love her. She does not meet strangers. I met her when I went to work in the Roosevelt School District, Roosevelt, New York. We are now retired, but we were junior high school social studies teachers. Like so many others, Jerrie and I have faced life's ups and downs (births, deaths, marriages, illness, etc.) together. We rely heavily on each other. She has a sense of humor and we find a reason to laugh whenever we meet. Jerrie's life is a celebration. She loves to try to make the best of any of life's situations, and she has the appropriate assignment, Sunshine Committee, where she is a part of a dynamic duo with Suzanne Rupert.

Mary Portis

Mary is my "Twin," we have so much in common. As natural look-alikes, students and others sometimes get us confused. We were both teachers, active in our churches and in the community. Everyone needs a Mary in their lives. She can do many things: organize activities, handle business affairs, care for the sick, and my favorite, an excellent travel partner. Mary is a woman of compassion and wisdom, and is a loyal, dedicated friend. It has been my privilege to work with her in day school, night school, and also I watched her transfer into the business world and back to the school community. She is truly my younger sister. The word "balance" comes to my mind when I think about Mary. We can literally discuss any subject, and I can rely on her to come up with a solution and also to see the "Big Picture." We are connected in the church, family, and the community.

Juanita Whitfield

Who is she and what does she mean to you? Everyone who knows her would have a different answer. Her children would probably tell you funny stories about their childhood. Her old friends have memories from the "Good Ole Days." Her pastor could tell you about her loyal, dedicated commitment to the church. My story concerning this lady is one of first admiration. I met her and got to know her after I had heard about her from a distance. We met one day in the old Bohack Supermarket on Greenwich Street in Hempstead, New York. I invited her to a "Copper Party," on the same night. She came and we became instant friends. We were both raising children alone. She had more experience and I did not understand some of her logic in the beginning, however, over the years, I embraced everything that she was trying to teach me. I am most proud to say that I observed her independence and the need to prepare for a rainy day. She continues to live her life in such a manner. She is one of the best friends that anyone could have. I have one "beef" with her: she spoiled my granddaughter, Talia. Oh! I forgot that she spoiled Allen too, who is Talia's father. Both of us attended Molloy College;

I graduated in 1978 and began my career in education; she graduated with a degree in social work and established a career with non-profit corporations. In retirement, we enjoy shopping, traveling and hanging out with our grandchildren.

Marion Fleming

One of the most well-known persons in Nassau County and beyond. She is a retired administrator from the Roosevelt school district. She began her career as an English teacher. We went through a very interesting time of testing while we were still working. As dedicated, skilled and talented persons, we worked under pressure for a short period of time, but the outcome was in our favor. Marion is a deaconess at the Union Baptist Church in Hempstead, New York. She remains active in her community: League of Women Voters and Roosevelt Retirees Organization. After retirement, Marion taught on the college level for many years. She also taught the AARP Driving Course for many years. She has been a member of the AKA Sorority for over fifty years.

Elaine Voss

"Friend" is what I call this wonderful lady. Dedication, loyalty, and compassion are just a few of the attributes that come to my mind when I think of Elaine. She came to the Roosevelt Junior- Senior High School as a science teacher. She was next door to me for a few years. She was concerned about the "whole child." Many of our students had needs outside of the academic realm. She was on the front line to help in any way that she could. Her students remember her with deep affection and reach out to her through social media.

Brother
Bishop J. Raymond Mackey is the founder of the Tabernacle of Joy Church, Uniondale, New York. He befriended my parents, Deacon William and Mother Cornelia H. Watson during the 1970s. They spent time in New York and he was a young pastor starting out in ministry. He continues to strive to make our communities better. He is the founder of HEVN: Helping End Violence Now.

Daughters

Najah Abdullah Smith,
Najah came into my life as an eighth-grade student. It was an instant connection. She was very mature for her age and I admire girls who believe in themselves. She was helpful in the classroom and she is a natural born go-getter. As the biological mother of boys, I welcomed Najah, who brought her entire family into my life. Included also was her grandmother, Ernestine, who insisted that I call her by her first name. (That was a no-no for people in my generation). Daily this young lady is proving herself as a talented businesswoman. She can be seen in her advertisements for Black Pop Up Markets, which consists of all types of vendors at various locations. My favorite is "Banana Pudding," from one of the several food

vendors. I am still in <u>awe,</u> as I remember with pride my young student, who is now making a difference in the lives of others.

Rev. Ellen Canty McEachern

She has lots of energy and unconditional love for me. In 1999, I became an assistant principal in the middle school. We went from the junior high school to the middle school model. Ellen was one of the two school nurses. The district was always in transition and she came to the pre-kindergarten while we were in the Harry Daniels Building, our third location. The things that we had in common were interesting: we share the same birthdate, August 16, with a fourteen-year separation; she was born in Wilmington, North Carolina; her mother was in the graduating class with my aunt, Alice Hansley Johnson; and we are both ministers. She was an asset to the staff and students. She is one of the most compassionate persons I know. Ellen is a scholar and she recently completed her doctoral studies. She is married to Rev. Richard O. McEachern, pastor of the Macedonia African Methodist Episcopal Church, Flushing, New York. They are the parents of two children, Richard Jr., and Nia.

Apostle Katherine Williams,

Chief Prelate of Refuge Alliance Ministries, pastor, teacher, and preacher are some of the titles that she is known by. We refer to her as our daughter. She is a kind, generous and compassionate person who spends much of her time visiting seniors and the sick. She will always be remembered by many as the leader of the distribution of food and other commodities after the devastation left by Hurricane Sandy in 2012. Her church, the House of Refuge, Baldwin, New York, was the distribution station.

Apostle Kendra Manigault

Pastor Kendra came into my life while working as a substitute teacher in the Roosevelt School District. Later she covered a class in the Roosevelt Pre-Kindergarten. We made an instant connection. She is concerned about my well-being and we communicate daily through Facebook. The most interesting fact is that we were a part of the same circles. She has the same birthdate as her godfather, Larry E. Mays. Kendra and her husband visited with me while I was visiting the family in Georgia. My favorite activity is making surprise appearances when she is in my area. She is known for her really nice gifts, hats, eyeglasses, and flowers.

Apostle Thelma Johnson

Pastor, loyal, dedicated, committed daughter and pastor of Rehoboth Fellowship Church of Hempstead. She is the dean of the HOR Bible School and she is also a businesswoman who has dedicated her life to God and to making the lives of those around her better. This young lady is a mover and shaker. She began as a student in Bible study and has been consistent in the ministry. She is a team player, who has survived some of the storms of life. She seeks to serve the community daily, and also has a thriving food pantry as a part of the local ministry.

Apostle Delores Copeland

Pastor of New Birth Deliverance Church, Brooklyn, New York. She is dedicated and loyal to the Body of Christ. She is on the front line for ministry. She shows her love for God by her daily life. She is a true example of Christ. Her commitment to Mother Apostle Callie Jasper is just one of her acts of kindness. She has supported me personally when I preached at the Greater Temple of Blessings, and also came to my birthday celebration. She is a member of the LI Conference of Clergy. She is also one of the favorite preachers for the Saint John Baptist Church of Westbury.

Doris Simeona

Administrative Assistant Doris was transferred to the high school after working in the Centennial Avenue School during the tenure of two principals. She was my secretary for five years. She began her career in the district after high school. She is a very ambitious lady who also attended beauty school and later graduated from Adelphi University. Doris and a team of others fixed many problems before they reached my desk.

Patricia Gordon

My beautiful, talented daughter is thoughtful and a true missionary. She is a talented musician and she loves to travel. She lives by the Bible: Love thy neighbor as thyself. She has a special place in her heart for children, especially Jasmine West. Pat and her mother, Althea, are very special family members who join us often in worship and they are supportive of our ministry. Their latest show of kindness love and generosity was when Jasmine came across the field after her graduation was over and discovered that they were there. Jasmine lives in Kannapolis, North Carolina.

Caprice Johnson

Caprice has a passionate love for people. While working in the health care field, she is known to be able to cut through the red tape and solve the problems. She is a student of the Word and is presently excited about her upcoming graduation from Bible school. Caprice has a strong desire to start a child-care program and is presently writing a business plan. She is active in her church and she loves outreach ministry.

Akousa Ageyman

Teacher. I drew my imaginary line with Akousa: "No more children." Every time I moved to a new assignment, someone would adopt me. While on my last assignment, Akousa was on my staff and she was whining about all of the responsibilities of a single parent. I laughed like Sarah and said to her, "Please do not go there." I remember when I joined the single moms. I also remember that I used that period in my life to seek a better life for me and my children.

Cheryl P. Augustine

Cheryl is an administrative assistant and also a former teacher who does not meet strangers. She taught me a valuable transforming lesson about love beyond the biological lines. I remember how and when she came into my life with her transparent charm and unconditional love for me. I have watched her face life's challenges head on and hold on to her faith in God.

Angela Hudson

Angie, as she is affectionately called, is a former student; class of 1990. She is now the principal of Ulysses Byas School, Roosevelt, New York. She is one of my first daughters in school. "Mommy" is her name for me. She began her teaching career in Roosevelt but later moved on to become a principal in another district. Angela has deep roots in the Roosevelt School, church and also the community.

Mae Geddis

Administrative assistant. I think of Mae Mae as my go-to daughter. No matter what the problem, I can call Mae and she can fix it. Her title is administrative assistant and she works in the Washington-Rose School. She has worked in the district since graduating from high school. It was my joy to attend her college graduation in 2017. She is also an active Member of Zion Cathedral in Freeport, New York.

Valleri Brown

Assistant teacher. This young lady, while small in stature, was a force to be reckoned with as a student. However, it was my gift to win her over with my no-nonsense manner. Valleri has a lot of energy and she can function in many capacities. She is very good with challenging students.

Josietta A. Johnson

"Godmother" is Nita's title for me. She makes me so proud because she has my work ethic. Employment is a life-changing experience. Most of the time, she has more than one job. She is a strong young woman and a recent cancer survivor. She faces life head on and has survived some of the storms of life. She is totally committed to ministry and to her family. She is creative and she has her own business.

Verona Green Miles

"Mama Mays" is Verona's reference me. She is a very organized, compassionate special education teacher. She was a member of my middle school staff and it was a real pleasure for me to observe her and to see her effective teaching skills. My favorite memory of Verona was a time when my Facebook page was hacked. I was attending a wake at Zion Cathedral in Freeport, New York, and another one of my former students sent me a message through public notification. I left the wake and went to a church service in Hempstead, New York, which is fifteen to twenty minutes away. Before I could get to Hempstead, quick thinking Verona used wisdom to shut the hacking down by using a test question, because she does know me. She concluded with the answer, "That is not my Mama Mays." Thus the hacking was ended.

Over the years, I have been honored to encounter many students, and I felt that God had blessed me and that He had shown His favor over my life through those students. I cannot mention everyone, but a few more stand out in my mind.

They are Nia Johnson, Kindalin Lowe, Lauran Mitchell and the Mitchell family, and Sharon and Shannon Hall. There was also another very special colleague, Debra Cavanagh, who worked with me in all areas to provide students with whatever they needed, whether it was volunteer tutoring or serving as an advisor.

It became a pattern that every time I got a new assignment, my extended family grew larger. When I came out of retirement and began my assignment as director of the Hi Hello Child Care Center, I was adopted by a very bright, creative, skilled and beautiful young lady, Meilee Bartley, who was one of the parents. Meilee is very visible and helpful to me in ministry.

Chapter 6

HEALTH CHALLENGES

I n 1974, I was accepted at Molloy College, and was sched-
uled to begin a month-long summer program. At that time,
I discovered a lump in my breast. It was very hard to study
and remain focused. However, I was able to make the necessary arrangements to have the lump removed. The lump
was benign. Later on I had another scare, and that lump was
also benign.

In 1995, my doctor discovered a growth under my left
chin. He treated me for over a year for a swollen gland, but
it kept growing, so he recommended surgery. In 1997, I had
the surgery and the tumor was much larger than previously
thought. My sisters, Marion and Audrey, were at my bedside
when the doctor informed them of the size of the tumor. The
news was not good. The tumor was cancerous. The good news
was that the surgery was successful. I had seven weeks of radiation with very little discomfort and was able to teach summer
school in Elmont, New York, that summer.

One small, but significant fact has been omitted. Bishop William A. Watson Jr., Dr. Phyllis Young, and other saints prayed the prayer of faith for me and the Lord raised me up. My long-time medical consultant, Rosalyn Johnson, who is a registered nurse, walked me through the entire process. At the end of the summer, while on vacation in Virginia, I was hospitalized for five days and was closely monitored because of my serious health issue. I returned home, went back to work, and was promoted several times. Thirteen years after surgery for the removal of a cancerous tumor and radiation, I retired in June 2011. Since retirement, I have continued to enjoy a very busy life as an assistant pastor to my brother, Bishop William A. Watson Jr., at the Saint John Baptist Church of Westbury, New York.

In 2003, I had a hysterectomy with no complications. My recovery allowed me to move around at a surprising pace for a person of my age. I was warned to slow down, but again, faith and prayer dominated my life. Mother Ophelia Simeona reminded everyone that the saints had prayed for speedy recovery.

In 2008, on a Friday morning, I arrived at work at the Washington-Rose Elementary School and could not get out of my car. Mrs. Helen Clemens, a parent, was looking out of the window and observed that I was having mobility issues. That was the beginning of knee problems. My treatment consisted of cortisone shots, but the relief only lasted for a short time, and I experienced much discomfort. While living with the bad knee, in November 2009, I was hit by a car while on my way to church. This time, I had surgery on my right knee.

Although the recovery period was lengthy, the surgery was a success, and I was literally given a new lease on life.

On November 4, 2010, while preparing to attend the pastor's installation banquet for the Free Will Baptist Church, I received a phone call from my primary care physician, informing me that I had breast cancer. Even though I was distraught, I was able to attend the function. After a second opinion from a cancer specialist and a breast MRI, it was determined that although there were aspects that required follow-ups annually, I did not have breast cancer. Eventually, I requested a new primary care physician.

Hand Surgery

I began to have a problem with my right-hand thumb. After several visits to the doctor, I was given a shot in my hand. It felt good for at least a year, but when the problem returned, I was referred to a hand specialist. After successful surgery, I have not had a problem. My hand is brand new.

In 2009, while having trouble with my legs, I was getting ready to retire. I was trying to decide whether to go on disability, and in the process I began to write letters and to do what I needed to do to get the process moving. Also, at that time I was transitioning from pre-kindergarten. The district said because they disbanded Pre-K, I had to go back to the middle school. I did not want to go back to middle school; I was just ready to retire. While getting ready to do that, I had to have interviews with the administration, and I did not consider that the interviews went very well. I do feel that some seeds of discord had been planted. However, while talking to the legal representation for the administrator's union, the legal team negotiated with the district to let me retire early. One day, I was having lunch at the Imperial with my godson, Dr. Ira Gerald, when I received a call from the administrative lawyer, and I was told that I had to go back to the middle school. I went back on a Wednesday and when I came out of the building on Wednesday, I asked the lawyer, "Get me out of here as soon as you can."

Well, this is what happened. I stayed Thursday and Friday, and by Friday I changed my mind. I knew then that my work was not over. To me, teaching and education are a calling. I had some unfinished business. I met some of the same young people I had encountered while the Pre-K was housed in the Washington Rose School. When Dr. Wright was away, the administrative assistant would ask for my help with students with discipline problems. My twenty-year career in middle school prepared me to deal with most problems. Consequently, my transition back to middle school was smooth because I already knew some of the students. As usual, with me, I began to enjoy my work.

Then only after a few weeks on the job, I had the misfortune of being struck by a car on November 10, 2009, in Baldwin, New York, at the corner of Seaman and Grand Avenue. I was on my way to church. Fortunately, I was eventually okay after three months of recovery, and surgery on my knee and therapy. I returned to work, but stated that I intended to retire in June 2010. I was encouraged to remain on the job longer. I agreed to do so, and I stayed a year longer and I retired on June 30, 2011.

The staff at the Roosevelt Middle School gave me a wonderful send-off. Included were some very nice gifts and vouchers for a Carnival Cruise. On February 6, 2019, I flew to Jacksonville, Florida, to finally go on my cruise. It was filled with wonderful memories, and most of all I am grateful to have been a part of such a kind, caring, and generous team. My career was filled with many memorable moments and individuals. Middle school students require a special understanding from all adults who are assigned to deal with them. When I reflect on my time spent with that age group, I still smile and say, "Thanks for the memories," especially to the graduating classes of 1990 and 1996 from the Roosevelt High School. I was the advisor for those classes.

My last two years were some of the most productive of my career. I had a chance to look in the rear-view mirror of life. I began as a substitute teacher and was eventually hired as a social studies teacher. I also taught adult education at night. Teaching adult education is extremely rewarding. I would begin each new session by telling my new students that I returned to school at thirty-two years of age to pursue a college degree. I also explained that adult students have a different set of problems than the traditional student. I tried to encourage them to persevere and to stay focused.

In 1999, I became an assistant principal with Ricardo Brown and another assistant principal. It was wonderful experience. From teacher to administrator was quite a transition. I was now in a leadership role. I never forgot the unpleasant experiences that I had as a teacher, and I did not repeat the undesirable behavior toward the staff. Consequently, I never had a grievance brought against me during my entire time as Administrator.

Conclusion

My cousin, Diane, who lives in California, called me in March 2018 to inform me that one of my mother's only two surviving sisters, Alice Johnson, was slipping away into eternal rest. Plans were made to return to Wilmington, North Carolina, where the wake and funeral were held. Although the trip was bittersweet, we were all happy to be together as a family. My brother, Cornelius, met us at the airport and we made the 136-mile trip to Wilmington. During the return trip to the airport, my niece, Loretta, asked me why I was not bitter about some of the things that happened to me in my life. I asked her to let me explain, and she sat quietly for at least thirty minutes while I talked. At this point, I shall repeat some of the ideas I have previously shared.

In January 1970, I became a single parent. I was already the mother of two boys and had learned that I was pregnant with number three. I do not remember being emotional or becoming depressed. I only knew two things: (1) The children were my responsibility and (2) God was on my side, according to the teachings of my parents. My decision was to keep moving. Yes, I shed a lot of tears when I was alone and asked many questions. How could a serious, hardworking, church girl like me end up in such an unfortunate predicament? But this was not the end of the story.

Nothing in my background while growing up in Virginia would have led anyone to believe that I would reach the level of accomplishments I have managed to attain. It is a long way from a woodpile in Virginia to an administrative office in Roosevelt, New York. As I explained to my niece, Loretta, I began in 1984 with a salary of $14,223 per year and retired with a very comfortable income provided by New York State United Teachers and Social Security. Nothing can erase all of the misfortunes that one will face in life, but if one can remain focused and listen and pay attention to that small voice that always guides us in the right direction, success is inevitable.

Now, Loretta, do you understand why I refused to let life's circumstances make me bitter? I chose to become better.

And Sarah laughed...

Life's Lessons to be shared

On February 1, 2015, the Saint John and Free Will Baptist Churches Women's Ministries presented a panel. The subject was "Stuck in a Rut." The speakers shared specific life experiences:

1 A mother navigated her way through the complicated school system trying to ensure the best for her special needs child. The information gained through her journey was invaluable. She shared that had she not been active in her child's education, the child would have fallen through the cracks, as it is with so many children.

2 A mothers shared the pain of losing her adult son after a long battle with diabetes.

3 A successful businesswomen suffering from a degenerative eye condition shared her feelings and her success story.

4 A mothers shared her experiences as the mother of a forty-year-old Down Syndrome son. She took us step by step as she used her experiences in a positive manner.

5 A mother of five children described her life in an abusive relationship. She developed a plan of escape in which she packed up her home and left within an hour and never looked back.

*****

All of the above scenarios are real, and I am a friend or acquaintance of all parties. All of these situations are within the confines of my story, **And Sarah Laughed.** All of those persons faced situations that could have turned out differently. What are the lessons that I would like the reader to learn?

1. Where there is life there is hope; one must open to receive help from others.
2. It is all right to become transparent. Seek professional help when necessary.
3. There is always a way out of any situation or condition.
4. Patience is a vital part of the process.
5. Stay focused and keep your eyes on your goals.
6. Seek positive energy.

7. Keep your purpose as your top priority.
8. God's timing is always perfect.

Sarah was sure that at her age, motherhood was impossible. With God, all things are possible. In our lives, we can recall times and situations when our future looked bleak. That is the way that I felt as a young, unskilled, abandoned, pregnant mother. I had done all the right things. I was married, attended church on a regular basis, and shared my meager resources with others. This was not a pretty picture. I only saw to the corner.

Jeremiah 9:11 says: *For I know the plans that I have for you...*

It was not possible for me to imagine that I could have come out of such a dark place in my life. Not only did I come out, but my life changed the face of my immediate family and also my extended family. Young people share with me that they are trying to be like me, and I am honored. Today I am living the life that I never imagined: retired, married to a loving gentleman, resources that allow me to seed generously to ministry, travel for ministry and pleasure, and I still love to cook and write the newsletter for my retirees' organization. Is there anything too hard for God? As I am writing, I remember the agony, pain, hurt, and loneliness of that young woman in her twenties, who went to the altar for prayer and returned home still hurting with a sense of hopelessness. I wore the mask well, and never told anyone how I was feeling.

I am not sure when I was fully recovered, but today, I almost feel as though I am referring to someone other than myself. My positive role model was my mother, Cornelia H. Watson, a lady with a physical disability, which she never allowed to impede her progress in life. She had only one eye due to a childhood accident. Mother was a scholar who loved to learn and she was my one-person fan club, who encouraged me to aim high. She always praised me for being successful in the completion of higher education. I will never forget the joy of both of my parents when I graduated from college in 1978. I was the first person in my immediate family to get a degree. Just recently, my son, Harold, and his wife Saretha, watched their daughter, Ahteras (aka Corie), become the first graduate in their family. Therefore, she was my first grandchild to graduate from college.

The secret to my success is three-fold, and consists of work, family and church.

As I write this last portion of my story, I just lost one of my best friends, Juanita Whitfield, to cancer on May 8, 2019. She fought a good fight. I was in a rare moment for me, a very pensive mood. I really wanted to fall apart when I received a call from my younger brother, Cornelius. He reminded me that I had never been alone. Our parents raised us to trust God. My brothers and sisters gave me unconditional support. They gave me emotional and financial support. All family members helped me with my childcare needs. When the children were younger, they would spend two to three months in Virginia with my parents and other family members. That would give me a break and allow me to work and rest properly. It was hard, but I always had sufficient housing and transportation.

Life became better as the years rolled by. We moved back to Hempstead in 1973 to a home owned by my brother, William. That house has been a haven for the family and others.

END NOTES

[1] So Sarah laughed to herself as she thought, After I am worn out and my lord is old, will I now have this pleasure?" Genesis 18:12, New International Version

[2] The righteous shall flourish like the palm tree: he shall grow like a cedar in Lebanon. Those that be planted in the house of the Lord shall flourish in the courts of our God. They shall still bring forth fruit in old age; they shall be fat and flourishing; Psalm 92:12-14 King James Version

[3] 12 Then Isaac sowed in that land, and received in the same year an hundredfold: and the Lord blessed him. Genesis 26:12 King James Version

[4] Food Rationing; History.com Editors. Food Rationing in Wartime History. History. June 1, 2019 https://www.history.com/news/food-rationing-in-wartime-america

[5] Greensboro Four; History.com Editors. Greensboro Sit-ins,. History. June 1, 2019.

https://www.history.com/topics/black-history/the-greensboro-sit-in

[6] I will bless the Lord at all times and His praises shall continually be in my mouth

Psalm 34:1 King James Version

[7] Headstart Program; U.S. Congress, An act to mobilize the human and financial resources of the Nation to combat poverty in the United States. (The Economic Opportunity Act) Act of 1964, S.2642, 88th Cong., introduced July 23, 1964.

[8] H.E.O.P. (Higher Education Opportunity Program). Elementary and Secondary Education Act (ESEA) Act of 1965, H.R. 2362, 89th Cong., introduced April 11, 1965